When I Grow Up, I Want To Be Like Daddy!

Story: Yusuf Ajaga
Illustrations: Dwayne 'DMAC' Mactavious

Text copyright © Yusuf Ajaga, 2024
Illustrations copyright © Dwayne Mactavious, 2024
Background patterns: Vecteezy.com

For more information contact: askthebookauthor@gmail.com

This book is dedicated to all dads
trying their best to be present
and to every child with an imagination
to encounter endless possibilities
but most importantly to the uniqueness
every child brings to the world
by being their authentic selves.

THIS BOOK BELONGS TO

_____

My name is AJ and when I grow up I want to be like my daddy!

He's the best doctor you've ever seen!
I could be a surgeon, working side by side.
We'd be the best team!

Maybe a paramedic, dentist, nurse,
or radiographer,
taking x-rays with my machines,
I'd be the coolest photographer!

When I grow up I want to be smart like my daddy!

I could be a teacher, perhaps a lawyer or a judge. I'd fight for an even justice system in court!

A firefighter, a policeman or I could even join the army. I'd get a soldier dog and name him Archie!

When I grow up I want to be sporty and fit like my daddy!

I could be an Olympian, a boxer, a wrestler or a bodybuilder!

Play football, volleyball, and basketball too! Wear my favourite Jordan's and my jersey will be blue!

When I grow up I want to dress like my daddy!

He has suits in many styles and colours and tonnes of shoes; maybe I could design a few.

If I were a model I'd pose like him too, show all 32 teeth like the cool guys do!

***When I grow up I want to speak like
my daddy!***

He uses big words; he's an eloquent speaker,
Maybe I could be a TV presenter!

Perhaps run for Mayor...Council...PM
Great major speeches, I'll get to make them!

When I grow up I want to cook like my daddy!

He makes a superb roast and is unmatched on the grill!

I could grow our food or catch it for the thrill!

When I grow up I want to be a cool driver like my daddy!

I could drive a formula one racing car and win first place!

And if I come 2nd or 3rd, daddy said he'll still love me for attempting the race!

I could be a bus driver, a train driver or even a pilot!

When I get clearance for take-off
I'd "whoosssshhhhhh" into the sky and smile when the sky turns violet.

When I grow up I want to be a handyman like my daddy!

I could be a carpenter; together we could make a toy train that goes choo-choo!
Or a chair, a rocking horse or a coffee table for brew!
Or I could be a surveyor or an architect and design buildings too!

When I grow up I want to have rhythm like my daddy!

He's a great dancer and he sings too!
Maybe I could be an artist and write the songs he'd dance to!

I could learn to play the bass guitar
and he could play the drums.
We would have so much fun!

When I grow up I want to be creative like my daddy!

I could have my own business or be a baker or buy stocks from the market just like my daddy.

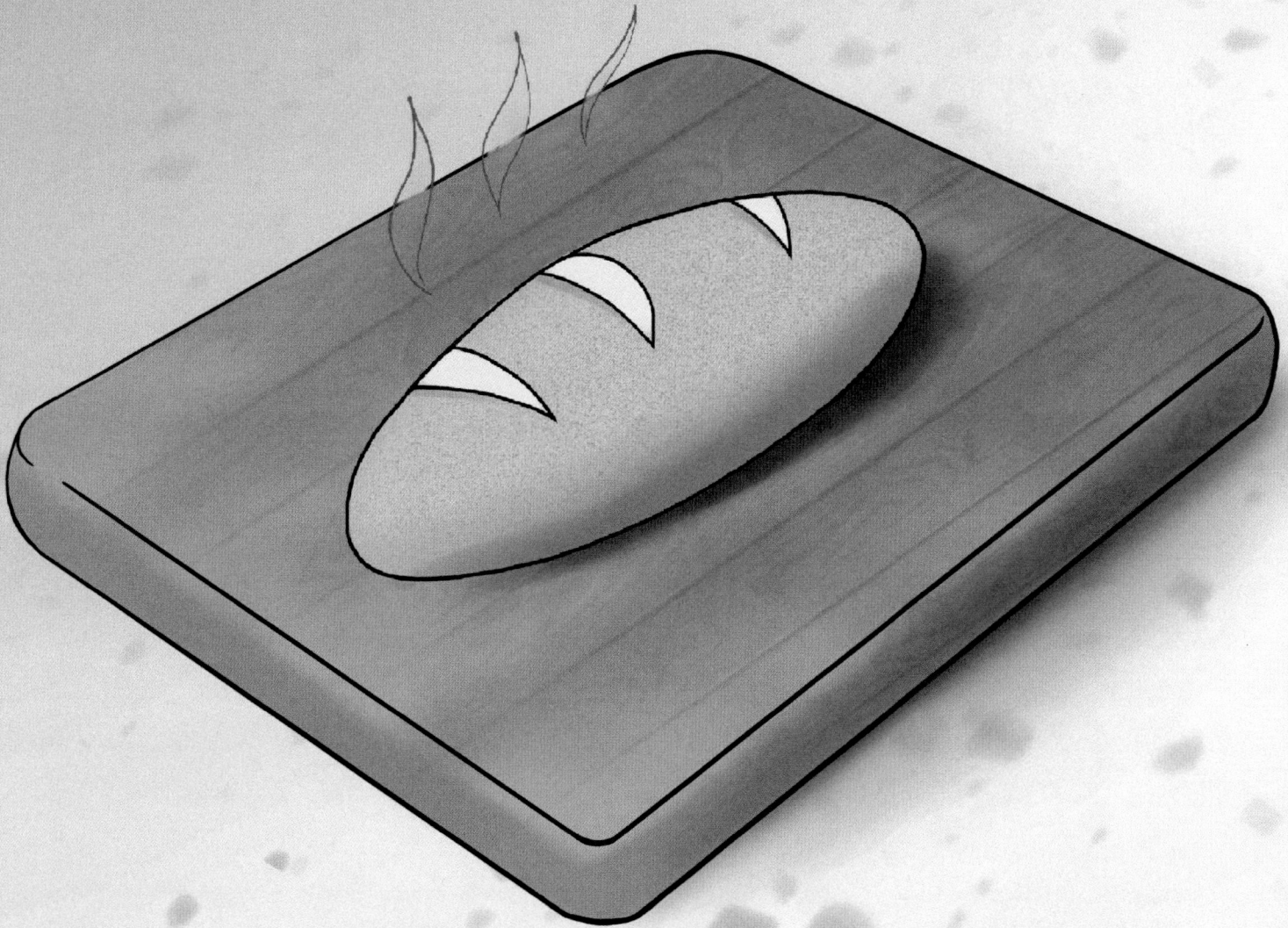

When I grow up there are many things I can be!

Daddy says there is time to choose and I should start by choosing to be "ME!"

THE END

Made in the USA
Monee, IL
13 June 2025

19327851R00019